BECOME REALLY

EFFECTIVE ON

TWITTER

IN JUST 5 DAYS

2014 EDITION

Also by Andrew Knowles

How to Write an Outstanding CV

Become Really Effective on LinkedIn

in Just 5 Days

BECOME REALLY EFFECTIVE ON

TWITTER

IN JUST 5 DAYS

2014 EDITION

UPDATED AND EXPANDED

You'll be tweeting

like an expert

in just five days

ANDREW KNOWLES

@andrew_writer

Contents

Introduction

This simple guide will help turn you from a Twitter novice into a confident tweeter.

How do I know that? Because I've seen it work for others.

Twitter is one of the least complicated communication systems on the planet. It allows you to send short messages across almost the entire world.

It's this simplicity that can be daunting, along with the uncertainty of whether you are 'doing it right'.

I began writing this book because, having trained people in how to use Twitter, I discovered that many were not putting what they had learned into practice. Worse, some were giving up Twitter entirely. I was curious to know why that was.

By asking lots of questions, I came to realise that for many people, learning how Twitter worked only solved part of their problem. What they wanted was someone to stand alongside them during their early days of tweeting. Someone who could suggest what action they should take next, and give them the reassurance that what they were doing was right.

Hence this book. It's grown out of a desire to give people the confidence they need to become highly effective tweeters. I hope it works for you too. While I started writing this book for those wanting to use Twitter in their business, the principles apply to any Twitter user.

The Twitter Action Plan began life as a short handout for training courses. It was so useful that it grew into a document several pages long that I gave away for free. From there it was a natural progression to create a short ebook, first published in early 2012. The 3rd edition has now been revised to include the new features introduced by Twitter in April 2014.

This is a Twitter learning aid

This short guide will help you get started with Twitter. It's a five-day action plan that takes you through different Twitter steps and helps you develop a Twitter routine.

If you already have a Twitter account, you can skip day zero, which is about how to set up your account from nothing. Although you may want to review it anyway, in case you've missed something.

This book is not a detailed training manual. It introduces you to the most important features of Twitter and helps you to remember them by encouraging you to use them over a five-day period.

It is like giving you a set of wooden blocks and showing you how to build with them. Once you know how to build, it is up to you what you make.

Once you're comfortable using the Twitter basics, you are free to explore some of the more advanced options in the back of the book, but you may find that you never need them.

Throughout this guide, you'll find lists of suggestions, tips and useful information, drawn from my own Twitter experience and that of the many other tweeters I have spoken with.

Twitter for business

If you're serious about growing your network of business contacts and increasing traffic to your website, you need to be using Twitter and other social media tools.

You can run and market your business without using social media. But online search tools, such as Google, are increasingly using social media 'mentions' and links when deciding how to rank sites. More and more business communication is occurring through social media channels – in some situations it's becoming a replacement for email.

In a few years' time, almost every business will be using social media, just as almost every business uses email today. Firms who don't want to move with the times will get left behind and most will eventually disappear.

By taking the time to master the basics of Twitter, and learning how to integrate it into your patterns of work, you are helping your business to stay relevant in today's fast-paced world.

INTRODUCTION

This book is for you if...

- You think Twitter could benefit your business, club, charity or other organisation, but you're not sure how.

- You're nervous about tweeting, because you don't want to get it wrong.

- You want to quickly build a network of interesting people.

- You don't know what to tweet about.

- You're bored of Facebook and want to experiment with something new.

- You don't know how often you should tweet.

- You're simply curious about Twitter.

- You work from home and want some virtual 'office chit chat' to break up your day.

- You want to find out whether Twitter is as much fun, or as useful, as you've been told it is.

Case study one: @purpledognet

A small business based entirely on Twitter

The Purple Dog Network is both a small business networking facilitator and a Twitter support and consultancy business.

It was founded by Alison Perry in June 2011 and now has over 57,000 followers, most of whom are small firms based in the UK.

Alison has a marketing background, but left that world a while ago and was looking for a business opportunity that fitted in with her role as a mother in a rural location. She first dabbled on Twitter in 2009 but rarely tweeted and had few followers.

Two years later, she began tweeting more often, and then she says "it clicked what Twitter was really about and the potential it had for business".

Alison set up @Purpledognet to build a network of contacts for her husband's firm. In one month, she had gained 2,500 followers; in four months, 10,000. She had discovered the secret of successful tweeting.

Alison has since turned the Purple Dog Network into a business based entirely on Twitter. She earns income from sponsorship, training and Twitter account management. She is well-respected in the Twitter small business community.

How does @Purpledognet use Twitter?

Growing a large following of genuine followers takes time. Alison worked very hard, proactively engaging with small firms using Twitter to encourage reciprocal following and retweeting. By sharing others' tweets, she got noticed and got followed.

It didn't take long for firms struggling to reach a couple of hundred followers to realise that being retweeted by @Purpledognet exposed their name to thousands of potential new followers. They learned that as they shared more, they were shared more often by others.

Alison picks and promotes one of her follower businesses every day and also promotes a different sponsor each day. She's also set up the #PDChallenge where Twitter users are encouraged to follow 10 new users a day for a month, and she actively encourages tweeters to follow small businesses with low follower counts.

What's changed since 2013?

@Purpledognet was a case study in the previous, 2013, edition of this book. The big change in Alison's approach to Twitter since then is that she now manages Twitter accounts for clients. She's an advocate (as am I) of small firms doing their own tweeting, but the reality is that some don't have the time and they're willing to pay for their account to be managed by someone with more experience.

Alison organised her first tweetup in 2013 - a meeting of her Twitter friends and followers, allowing them to put names to faces, shake hands and exchange stories and tips.

How do you choose who to follow on Twitter?

Alison follows small businesses from across the UK. She takes a moment to assess each account before following, checking to see whether they have a profile picture and a bio. If they don't, or if their most recent tweets include offensive content, they won't be followed.

A bio stuffed with hashtags or references to #teamfollowback and the like are also unlikely to get a follow from @purpledognet.

Key statistics for @Purpledognet	
Twitter account opened:	2 June 2011
Number of followers:	Over 57,800
@Purpledognet follows:	Over 31,600
Number of tweets sent since June 2011:	Over 61,500
Average number of tweets per day:	63

Day zero

Yes, there is a day zero. This is the day given over to setting up a brand new Twitter account. If you already have an account, you can skip this and go directly to day one, although you may want to check that you haven't missed anything.

Step 1: Go to twitter.com or run the Twitter app on your mobile device.

You can create an account from your computer, smartphone or tablet computer.

Step 2: Enter your details.

Enter an email account that you have access to, as you'll need to respond to a verification email. Choose a user name that you like the sound of.

Twitter allows you to change both the email address and the user name as often as you like, so don't be concerned about this being a really important one-time choice, because it isn't. I'll explain how to choose a good user name later.

You can only link one email account to one Twitter account.

It may be that you opened a Twitter account months, or even years, ago, using your main or favourite email address and now you can't remember the password or even the name of the Twitter account. Twitter will prevent you from re-using that email address with a new account.

But don't despair if you can't remember the details of an account you created some time ago - there's an easy way to recover the situation. Go back to Twitter.com and in the 'Sign in' section, type your email address into the field marked 'User name or email'. Then click the 'Forgot password?' option below. Twitter will send a message to your email address, allowing you to change the password and recover your old account - or to delete it, if you want to start again.

As part of the initial sign-up, you're agreeing to the Twitter Terms of Service. You probably won't read these (who does?) so I've added a summary of the key points at the end of this chapter.

Step 3: Get through the opening steps.

Twitter now takes you through a series of steps designed to teach you some basics and help get your account running.

As part of the introduction, Twitter suggests celebrities and other major accounts for you to follow, and invites you to search for contacts based on your email address book.

I recommend that you skip through this process as quickly as possible. Don't worry if Twitter forces you to follow a few celebrity accounts as part of the set-up process - you can unfollow them later.

Press 'next' or 'skip' when you get a chance. The 'skip' or 'next' option is a button or a link somewhere on the page, and it may be quite small and hard to spot, at the bottom of one of the boxes on the page.

It's no surprise that some celebrities have millions of followers, when Twitter effectively forces new users to follow them as part of the sign-up process.

Twitter will also ask to search through your email contacts in a bid to connect you with people you might know who are already on Twitter. This requires you to give Twitter access to your contacts, by clicking a button that grants permission. It's your choice whether you do this, or just skip this step.

Step 4: Add character to your new account.

As part of the set-up process, Twitter asks you to upload a profile picture and write a short bio.

Your Twitter profile, the picture and text, is really important. Many tweeters will choose to follow you, or ignore you, based on these alone.

If you don't upload your photo now, or write a short bio, you can add these later.

Step 5: Send your first tweet.

Twitter is so keen for you to send your initial tweet that they've even written it for you! If you click on the **'Me'** option, you'll see a couple of pre-prepared tweets, saying something like: 'Just setting up my Twitter #myfirstTweet'.

If you want to send one of these, just press the **'Tweet'** button. If not, just ignore them.

Step 6: Confirm your email address.

If you haven't already done this, find the email that Twitter sent when you opened the account and click on the confirmation link. If you don't, you'll find that certain features can't be used in Twitter.

Step 7: Add a website address.

You've now completed the step-by-step process of creating a Twitter account, but there's more to do. Click on the cog or wheel symbol at the top right of the page and choose the 'Settings' option. Now select the 'Profile' tab (on the left).

Alternatively, if you have your profile page on the screen (that's the one you get by pressing 'Me'), click on the 'Edit Profile' button on the right, just below the header.

You can add a link to a single web page from your Twitter profile. It might be a link to your business website, your blog or your Facebook account. If you have more than one site that you want to link to, you can include the other links in your bio.

Step 8: Review your bio.

Here you summarise yourself in 160 characters. Be as creative, quirky or informative as you like. If you're not sure what to write, take a look at what others have written about themselves before creating your own.

Many Twitter users will read your bio before choosing whether to follow you. If your bio is missing, or too short to be informative, it may deter some people from becoming your followers. When you read the case studies in this book, you'll see that many business tweeters decide not to follow someone because their bio is missing or not meaningful.

You can add one or more website links in the bio box.

Step 9: Review your photo and upload a header.

This is really important. Tweeters get an instant impression of who you are from your profile picture and header image.

Your profile image is usually displayed as a tiny square on the screen of whatever device the tweeter is using to browse Twitter. Clear and simple are good rules when it comes to selecting a profile picture.

Twitter recommends using an image that is 400 x 400 pixels. But you can upload a larger image to Twitter and crop it to the area and size you want with the tools provided. The only restriction is that the file size must be less than 10Mb in size, which is quite large.

If you use an image that's less than the recommended 400 x 400 pixels, Twitter will inflate it to fill the space and it could appear pixelated, or blocky. So it's best to start with a larger picture and cut it down.

Before choosing an image to use, take a look at what other tweeters are using on their profiles. This will give you an idea of what looks good and what doesn't.

You can use a photo of yourself or something that represents the purpose of your Twitter account.

An eye-catching profile picture does just that and helps your tweets get noticed. Don't forget that every one of your tweets will be accompanied by the profile picture you have selected.

The header picture on your Twitter account is the big banner that runs across the top of your main Twitter page, which you can view by selecting the **'Me'** option. Unlike the profile picture, this banner is only visible on this page, but it will be seen by every tweeter who decides to take a look at your account. So again, it's important to choose carefully.

Twitter recommends a size of 1500 x 500 pixels for this image, but again, you can use a larger image and then choose to magnify and/or select the area you want to use. Use a small image and Twitter will inflate it, with the risk that it will appear blocky.

To see how your header and profile picture work together, click on the **'Me'** tab. The profile picture is the small square on the left, with the header around it.

When choosing a header image, remember that it may appear differently depending on what device you are using. On a tablet, the header is the background to your account name, bio and other details, all of which are displayed in white text. If you choose a header with a light colour, that text could become unreadable.

Some people get very imaginative in their combination of header and profile pictures. You can have fun with this, but don't get carried away. In reality, some Twitter users rarely, if ever, see this page, because they use other systems to read and write tweets.

Step 10: Explore the options under 'Settings':

The '**Account**' tab is where you can change the name of your Twitter account or your email address. As already mentioned, you can change both of these as often as you like. There are also a host of other options about language, location, sensitive material and the like. Take a moment to review these, so that you understand what you're choosing.

The '**Security and privacy**' tab lets you decide whether to make your tweets public or private and allows you to turn on two-step login verification and other privacy features.

The '**Password**' tab is self-explanatory – here you can change your password.

The '**Mobile**' tab allows you to download the Twitter app to your mobile phone, and to link Twitter to text messaging. You can also choose whether to receive tweets and notifications via text.

The '**Email Notifications**' tab allows you to choose whether you receive emails when certain events occur, such as when someone starts following you on Twitter. Just a word of caution. In my experience, these notifications don't always come through. The list of notification types is continually growing and more options are being added. You can also choose to receive various Twitter updates by email.

The **'Web Notifications'** tab allows you to choose whether you receive notifications in your web browser when certain events relating to your Twitter account occur. This is a new feature for 2014.

I've already covered the '**Profile**' tab above.

Under the **'Design'** tab, you can change the background design of your Twitter page. You can choose a premade theme or design and upload your own. Personally, I rarely visit Twitter pages, as I use other systems for managing my Twitter account, so I would not spend too much time deciding on a background choice.

In April 2014, Twitter started introducing a new look to their pages, which at the time of writing only applies to the 'Me' or main profile page. The background image is invisible in this new design and I expect this new look will be applied across the rest of Twitter in due course, entirely eliminating the background design.

The '**Apps**' tab lists the apps that you've given permission to access your Twitter account. These can include the Twitter app for iPhone, the app for connecting with Facebook and a host of other systems.

The '**Widgets**' tab makes it really easy to insert a stream of tweets onto your website. You can choose from a number of options, such as to show all the tweets from the timeline of a particular Twitter account, or all the tweets from members of a named list (I'll talk about lists on day four), or one of several other options. The widget tool then creates a piece of code which, when inserted into your website, displays the Twitter stream.

Summary of day zero

- You have created your Twitter account!

- You have created a basic profile, although you will probably begin tweaking it once you've been using Twitter for a short while.

- You have uploaded a profile picture.

- You have reviewed the other settings and perhaps changed a few things.

- You now have a functioning Twitter account and are ready for day one of 'Your Five-Day Twitter Action Plan'!

Summary of the Twitter Terms of Service

Before you start on day one, it's important to consider the terms under which you have agreed to use Twitter.

It's a bit of a joke that we all tick the box saying we agree with the terms of service, but very few of us actually read them.

The good news is that the Twitter terms are quite reasonable - you're not agreeing to them taking ownership of your prized possessions or to having the Twitter symbol tattooed on your forehead.

However there are some key points you should be aware of. I have summarised these below.

1. You are what you tweet. What you share on Twitter is your responsibility, and you will bear the consequences. Twitter says: "You should only provide Content that you are comfortable sharing with others under these Terms." By Content they mean words, images or video or anything else you can post within a tweet.

2. Get permission if you're tweeting for an organisation. If you're running a Twitter account for a company, club, charity or some other body, by accepting the terms, you're confirming that you have permission to represent that organisation.

3. Don't rely entirely on Twitter. It might not always be there. The service can be changed or stopped, permanently or temporarily, with no notice. If you are heavily dependent on Twitter, you need to think how losing access to Twitter could impact your business.

4. Points about privacy. Twitter collects and uses some of the information you supply, in accordance with their Privacy Policy. They may need to get in touch with you from time to time, but you can opt out of most communications from them.

5. Have a strong password. Twitter encourages you to use passwords "that include a combination of upper and lower case letters, numbers and symbols".

6. Twitter is not monitored. Actually, there are lots of people watching what gets said on Twitter. But the people who run Twitter make it clear they neither monitor nor control what's being said. As a result, Twitter warns that "you may be exposed to Content that might be offensive, harmful, inaccurate or otherwise inappropriate, or in some cases, postings that have been mislabelled or are otherwise deceptive".

7. Your tweet is always yours, but... You will always retain ownership of the words, sentences and images that you tweet (assuming they were yours in the first place, that is).

However, by agreeing to their terms, you grant Twitter "a worldwide, non-exclusive, royalty-free license (with the right to sublicense) to use, copy, reproduce, process, adapt, modify, publish, transmit, display and distribute such Content in any and all media or distribution methods (now known or later developed)".

Which, in short, means you're giving them permission to pass your tweet on to others.

8. Twitter won't pay you. Twitter, and its partners, can use the content of your tweets (including photos) without paying you a bean. But before you get angry about this, Twitter is very clear that you retain ownership over everything you post, and they have rules governing what their partners can and can't do with your content.

It's not in Twitter's interests to allow others to profit from what you tweet, without you getting a fair share. But neither is it their job to ensure you get paid. If you tweet a picture that finds its way to the front page of a national newspaper, it's your job to chase them up for credit and payment.

9. You'll be the one who goes to jail. In line with their policy that you own what you tweet, if you post anything that breaks copyright or other rules, you'll be the one who gets into trouble with the law.

10. You can't use the 'Twitter' name. Anything which clearly identifies Twitter (the word 'Twitter', logos etc.) belongs to them and you have no right to use it. Of course, products like this book need to carry the name to identify what they're about, but you can't do anything which might imply you're acting on behalf of Twitter.

11. Read the Rules. Certain behaviours are banned, or at least discouraged, on Twitter. To make sure you keep away from these, read the official Twitter Rules.

12. Twitter is for people aged 13 and upwards. In their Privacy Policy, Twitter says: "Our Services are not directed to persons under 13." If they discover an account is being run by someone under 13, they will deactivate it and delete all the data.

13. Your account can be turned off without notice. If Twitter decides that you're doing something they don't like, they can switch your account off without any warning.

Summary of the Twitter Rules

If you're using Twitter for a business or any other organisation, you should read the Twitter Rules in full for yourself. Here's a summary of the key points.

1. Don't impersonate others. Pretending to be a celebrity, a well-known brand or your next-door neighbour is not allowed, if you're intending to "mislead, confuse, or deceive others".

That's not to say you can't run a spoof account, but you should declare it as such.

2. Trademarks are protected. Twitter can reclaim or close accounts that use the trademarks, business names or logos of established organisations.

3. Don't publish private information. This includes home addresses, telephone numbers, email addresses and other forms of identification. Break this rule and you could find yourself on the wrong side of the law.

4. Don't make threats. The rules say: "You may not publish or post direct, specific threats of violence against others." Even if you do it in jest, making a threat on Twitter could get you into very serious trouble.

5. Respect copyright. "Twitter respects the intellectual property rights of others and expects users of the Services to do the same."

6. Don't open lots of accounts for the same purpose. It's fine to have more than one Twitter account, but make sure they have different purposes, otherwise they might fall foul of the Twitter spam rules and get closed down.

7. Not for sale. "You may not buy or sell Twitter usernames."

8. Don't spam. Twitter hates spammers and has a long list of criteria it uses to decide whether your activity constitutes spam. Using common sense should keep you clear of the anti-spam rules - don't bombard other Twitter users with constant sales plugs or misleading messages or use aggressive techniques to grow your followers quickly.

Case study two: @sas_stacey

Virtual PA turns Twitter into a marketing machine

Stacey Renphrey is a well-respected 'virtual PA' with a high profile on Twitter. Since late 2011 when she began freelancing, Stacey has been gaining recognition, winning awards and attracting new clients - all as a result of her tweets.

And yet, when she launched into self-employment, Stacey didn't know anything about Twitter and had no idea that it would quickly become the source of almost all her business income.

As a 'virtual PA', Stacey looks after administrative tasks on behalf of individuals and small firms who don't have the time to do it themselves. Using the internet and cloud computing, she can work for almost anyone, regardless of where they are based.

It was one of Stacey's very first clients who asked her to take a look at Twitter. Within six weeks of tweeting for herself, she'd secured another client via the social network. A couple of weeks later, she achieved the landmark of her first one thousand followers.

Since then, Stacey has won the Theo Paphitis Small Business Sunday award on Twitter and been approached to be a SAGE Business Expert. She says 95% of her work now comes through Twitter.

How does @SAS_Stacey use Twitter?

Stacey says of Twitter: "It's very much give and take." She began by giving a lot, quickly developing a reputation for retweeting others. She uses Twitter lists to keep track of the tweeters she likes to retweet often.

Online networking is at the heart of Stacey's Twitter strategy. She soon became involved in #purplebiz and #bluebiznet, giving her exposure to thousands of other Twitter users, most of whom are small businesses - her target market.

By planning ahead and making good use of scheduled tweets, Stacey ensures that her business presents clear, consistent messages every day, giving her time to engage in Twitter conversations as appropriate.

Blog posts are another important element in Stacey's strategy. By writing posts that are of interest to other firms, she creates a pool of resources to tweet about and that bring readers to her website.

While she posts a lot of tweets every day, you won't find Stacey talking about her family or home life on Twitter. She keeps her approach light-hearted but strictly business.

How do you choose who to follow on Twitter?

@SAS_Stacey follows tweeters who are active and who demonstrate support for others, particularly small businesses. She keeps up with some accounts by adding them to a list but not following them directly.

Key statistics for @SAS_Stacey	
Twitter account opened:	11 December 2011
Number of followers:	Over 5,400
@SAS_Stacey follows:	Over 4,200
Number of tweets since December 2011:	Over 46,900
Average tweets per day:	63

A change of direction in 2014

During 2014, Stacey's Twitter account changed its name to @SAS_Positivity and Stacey now uses it to promote her new project, 'The Positivity Diet', instead of her PA business.

Choosing your Twitter name

The name you adopt for your Twitter account can make a huge difference to how others think of it (and how they think of you).

To demonstrate this, what do these Twitter names bring to mind?

@marksandspencer
@BusyBeeCandles
@Beside_The_Sea
@amknowles

Three of these names probably inspire a clear image in your mind - a well-known retailer, a candle maker, a coastal scene and... what? The last name, @amknowles, is probably meaningless.

I originally called my Twitter account @amknowles because I was uncertain about what I'd use it for, so it made sense to use my initials and my surname. A few months later, I realised the name meant nothing to other Twitter users, so I changed it to @andrew_writer. This is more descriptive of who I am and what I do, making it easier for people to relate to me.

Of the other names above, you recognise one because it's a household brand, while another evokes images of softly glowing illuminations. The third stimulates thoughts of the seaside, whatever that might look like to you. (This account promotes self-catering accommodation and the choice of name is itself a strong sales message).

Because Twitter is a network powered more by text than images, the words you choose to describe your account are important.

Here are the main things to consider when choosing a name:

1. Your account name must be unique. As more and more people open Twitter accounts, it's becoming increasingly difficult to find names which are still available. The only characters you can use are letters, numbers and the underscore symbol '_'. Twitter does not distinguish between upper and lower case characters.

Don't be afraid to be imaginative in your use of the characters available.

2. Your account name can be changed as often as you like. But changing it could confuse your followers, particularly if you update your profile image at the same time. Names you stop using become available to other Twitter users. I no longer have control over @amknowles, which is now being used by someone else.

3. A good name summarises what your Twitter account is all about. My current account name says both who I am and what I do, whereas I felt the previous account name, while accurate, said very little to other Twitter users.

Think about the message or brand you want to promote through your Twitter account. Because I use mine to tweet both personal and commercial content, the name needed to span both.

4. You can create multiple Twitter accounts. Because every account has its own voice and message, you may need to operate more than one to address different audiences.

I set up my second Twitter account, @biz_oh, soon after opening my first. I wanted to regularly tweet business tips, news and links to my business blog (www.bizoh.net) without cluttering up my personal account. So it seemed logical to create a separate account, giving the blog its own voice.

This is acceptable under the Twitter rules, because the two accounts have quite different purposes.

Please note that other than quoting their names here, I have no affiliation with @marksandspencer @BusyBeeCandles or @Beside_The_Sea.

Day one

Plan to log into Twitter at least three times today. Ideally, in the morning, around midday, and sometime later in the afternoon or evening.

If you want to use Twitter to grow a network of contacts and uncover opportunities, you need to be reasonably active. Logging in at least once a day is really the minimum needed to be effective. Obviously there will be occasional days when it's not possible to log in at all, but try to aim for three times a day, at least to start with.

If finding time for Twitter from your computer is difficult, consider logging in from your phone or another mobile device. This also gives you the freedom to log in when you're away from your desk, such as when you're on public transport or outdoors. Many people tweet almost exclusively from a mobile device.

All the descriptions used in this book for navigating around Twitter refer to the computer-based version, which looks the same whether you're on a Windows computer or a Mac. The options for the mobile and tablet versions of Twitter are similar, but not identical.

Here's the routine for day one:

Step 1: Log into Twitter.

Step 2: Add some followers.

People that you might want to follow are:

- Your existing contacts who are also Twitter users.
- Organisations who supply information that you use (news, industry blogs etc.).
- Other professionals in your sector, who you discover through Twitter or other networks.
- Local people or businesses you find useful.
- Tweeters who send out messages that interest or amuse you.
- People referred to, or retweeted by, those you already follow.

There are several ways to find new followers:

- From Twitter account details supplied by your contacts.
- Find existing contacts who are on Twitter by using the **'Find friends'** tab on the '#Discover' page.
- Follow Twitter links from websites of individuals or organisations.
- On the '**#Discover**' page, click through the various tabs ('Tweets', 'Activity', 'Who to follow', 'Find friends' and 'Popular accounts') for ideas on who Twitter thinks may be interesting or relevant to you.

- Pick from the list of suggestions presented in various places by Twitter, based on its guess at what interests you. There is a short list on your homepage and a more detailed list under the '**Who to follow**' tab on the '#Discover' page.

Remember, it's entirely up to you who you follow on Twitter. You don't need a 'good reason' for following someone. People like to be followed.

When you follow someone, Twitter sends them an email telling them that they have a new follower. This option can be turned off, but many tweeters leave it on.

From now on, consider adding at least three to five new followers a day, but try to keep the total in balance with the number who follows you. There are different views on what is the best ratio of following to followers, so find the one that works for you.

Step 3: Take a look at tweets by those you've started following.

These give you a feel for how others are using Twitter. Go to the '**Home**' button (top left) to see the most recent tweets from those you follow. These give you a flavour of current topics or conversations.

Do not feel obliged to read every tweet sent by those you follow since you last logged in. Of course, you can if you want, and when you're only following a few people, it's quite easy to achieve. But Twitter is a 'real time' system, and no one expects you to read every message.

If you miss something, you miss it. If it's that good, it'll probably be repeated. If it's something that someone really wants you to know, they'll find a way of telling you. Using Twitter effectively means learning to live in the moment and not worrying about the tweets that have passed you by.

Step 4: Send a few tweets of your own using the quill icon - 'Compose new Tweet' button - at the top right of the page.

You may be wondering what to tweet about. This can be a big problem for many Twitter users, both newcomers and those who've been around for a while. You probably feel that you have nothing to say that's of any great significance.

One way to start is by taking a lead from what others are tweeting about. If this doesn't work for you, here are some other suggestions:

- Tweet about what's going on around you right now. It might be as simple as saying "I'm having a coffee" or "Taking the dog to the vet's this afternoon". These simple tweets give others an insight into your life.

But remember, Twitter is a public forum, so only talk about those things you are comfortable disclosing. Pause before pressing **'Tweet'**, to be sure you really want to send that message.

You can delete tweets after sending them if you change your mind, but someone may have already read them.

- Tweet about something you are looking forward to. Such as: "I'm going to the Business South West conference next week. I hope it's as productive as last year" or "Having a day out on Friday. Picnic by the sea. What could be better?"

- Tweet about your work. This is important for networking, because it helps your followers to understand what you do. But be wary of client confidentiality. I'm a writer, so I might tweet "I'm working through a stack of client blog posts today" or "It looks like I could soon be writing content for a website for a plumber's merchant".

But I never tweet "Just got off the phone from my most annoying client". Why? Partly because my clients may be following me on Twitter, but also because I don't want to give a bad impression to potential clients.

- Share interesting or relevant articles or pictures from other websites. Write a short tweet and paste the website address you are referring to into the tweet. Twitter will automatically shorten it.

Step 5: Send a few retweets or comments.

Tweeters love it when someone engages in conversation, whether it's a Twitter friend or a total stranger.

Don't be afraid of creating offence by commenting on tweets that others are sharing.

There are two ways you can join in with conversations: reply and retweet. Take a look at the options displayed beneath each tweet in your timeline.

The first option is '**Reply**'. If you click on this, you are presented with a box into which you can type a reply tweet that's addressed to the sender of the original tweet. You could compliment them on their tweet, ask a question, or share some extra information with them.

Your message will start with @twittername and the comment you make will be sent just to them, and to anyone who follows both you and them. Twitter is a public space - users expect others to comment on what they are saying. In fact, they like it. Your replies only appear in the 'Tweets and replies' timeline on your profile page.

The second option is to '**Retweet**'. A retweet (or RT) is where you forward a tweet written by someone else to your own followers. If you read something that makes you laugh, retweet it. If someone refers to an article that you think has some merit, retweet the message which contains the link.

Click on '**Retweet**' and Twitter will ask if you want to 'Retweet this to your followers?' Click on the '**Retweet**' button to retweet the message to your followers or '**Cancel**' if you have changed your mind.

Retweeting is a great way to share interesting, useful or humorous tweets. It can also be a good way to get noticed by the person who originally sent the tweet, because Twitter informs them of your retweet.

You can undo a retweet, simply by clicking on the retweet option. This removes the retweet from your timeline.

On the left below each tweet, you will see an invitation to 'Expand' or 'View'. Clicking on this shows you what else has already happened to this tweet, such as whether it's been retweeted or favourited by someone else.

An alternative way of communicating with another tweeter is by sending a **Direct Message**. You can usually only do this to someone who follows you. From your homepage, bring up your list of followers. Click on the cog icon to the left of the 'Follow' or 'Following' button to bring up a list of options, including 'Send a Direct Message'. This message only goes to that person and is private.

Once you have sent or received a direct message, that tweeter's details appear in the list of your direct messages which can be accessed via the envelope symbol at the top of the page.

Summary of day one

- You have added some followers.
- You have reviewed current conversations.
- You have reviewed comments by those you follow.
- You have sent a few tweets of your own.
- You have sent a few retweets or made some comments.

1 Twitter account you must follow

1. Follow @support. This is the official Twitter support account and tweets useful reminders and advice about potential problems. It doesn't tweet very often, but when it does, the tweets are worth reading.

2 checks before you tweet

1. Proofread your tweet. It might only be 140 characters, but that still leaves plenty of room for spelling errors and silly typos. One little mistake can entirely alter the meaning of your tweet. Some tweeters may even judge you by whether you use apostrophes correctly!

2. Do you really want the world to know what you're about to share? Think for a moment about how others might interpret your message.

Case study three: @madebylisaxx

Twitter converts a hobby to a business

Lisa Coles, from West Sussex, loves making jewellery. Encouraged by friends, she opened a Facebook page in January 2013 to introduce her creations to a wider audience.

To Lisa's surprise, she soon started getting orders. At that time, the jewellery making was very much a hobby for the full-time mother of three. However, the success on Facebook led her to open a Twitter account in February 2013.

This wasn't Lisa's first experience of tweeting, having previously used the network to follow celebrities. But now she was coming to Twitter with a clearer purpose and she started by Googling articles giving advice about using social networks for marketing.

Her next step was to begin following people already using Twitter to promote jewellery, to see how they went about it. Lisa also joined in with networking hours, all the time watching and learning from others. Within six weeks of joining Twitter she had over one thousand followers.

Today Lisa's hobby is a business run from home. She's adjusted her prices to a commercial level and is making profits. Her ambition is to open her own jewellery shop.

Twitter is Lisa's primary social network although she's also on Facebook, Pinterest, Google+ and LinkedIn. Four out of five of her sales are through Twitter.

How does @madebylisaxx use Twitter?

Lisa's Twitter success is based on active participation in networking groups. She's involved with @Purpledognet and @TeamFreddiePig, both of which help promote small businesses. She's also part of #twittersisters, a group of tweeters working hard to promote newcomers to the network.

From time to time, Lisa gives away an item of jewellery to one of her followers, as a way of encouraging them to retweet her posts and as a thank you for their support.

Having initially invested hours each day into Twitter, Lisa now spends just 60 minutes on her daily tweeting routine. She makes a point of thanking those who retweet her and uses Hootsuite to schedule messages across the time when she's not online.

How do you choose who to follow on Twitter?

As with almost every other tweeter profiled in this book, Lisa does not follow people who don't have a profile picture or a Twitter bio. She usually follows back if the tweeter represents a small business, but she wants their tweets to demonstrate evidence of engagement.

Key statistics for @madebylisaxx

Twitter account opened:	19 January 2013
Number of followers:	Over 9,200
@madebylisaxx follows:	Over 7,200
Number of tweets since January 2013:	Over 34,200
Average number of tweets per day:	102

A change of direction in 2014

During 2014, Lisa decided to put her successful jewellery business on hold in order to concentrate on other work commitments. Her Twitter account is no longer active.

Day two

As with day one, try to log into Twitter more than once during the day. If you're serious about wanting to build a following and a presence on Twitter, it takes time and commitment.

Step 1: Repeat steps 1-5 from yesterday.

- Log in.

- Add some new followers.

- Review current conversations and comments by those you follow.

- Send a few tweets.

- Send a few retweets or make some comments.

Step 2: Check whether anyone's replied to you or mentioned you.

To do this, click **'Notifications'** at the top left of the page. On the left you'll see two options – 'Notifications' and 'Mentions'.

'Notifications' is a list of all the contacts you've had with other tweeters. You can choose to filter the list to only show notifications from people you follow.

Notifications shows you:

• Who has followed you.

• Who has retweeted you.

• Who has favourited one of your tweets.

• Who has mentioned your Twitter name in their tweet.

• Who has added you to a public Twitter list.

Reviewing this list of Twitter interactions must be at the heart of your Twitter routine. It tells you who is engaging with you and these tweeters can become valuable contacts.

'Mentions' is simply a list of all the tweets by others that include your user name. This includes the replies and tweets where you have been 'mentioned', which are also included on the notifications tab, but excludes other items, such as new follower notifications and retweets.

If someone has retweeted one of your tweets, it's polite to reply to them with a short thank you tweet. If you've been asked a question or simply mentioned in some way, make an appropriate response.

Step 3: Review your followers.

Click on **'Home'** and then **'Followers'** on the top left of your screen and you'll be shown a list of people who follow you on Twitter. If you also follow them, a blue following button is displayed. Alternatively, click on **'Followers'** beneath the header on your profile page.

- **Decide whether you want to follow any of them back.** Look down the list. If someone's following you and you'd like to follow them back, just click the 'Follow' button. If you want to know more about them, click on their name to view their full profile.

- **Decide if there is anyone you want to block.** Every now and again you will gain a follower who you'd rather wasn't there for some reason. The way to stop them following you is to block them.

Press the little cog button, next to the follow or following button, and it gives you a list of options. One of these is the option to block them.

If you block someone in error, there is an undo option on their profile page.

Quick tip: you can force someone to unfollow you without leaving them blocked. Choose the **'Block'** option and they'll immediately be marked as blocked. Put the cursor over the **'Blocked'** button and it changes to **'Unblock'**. Click this and they're no longer blocked, but nor are they following you.

Step 4: Review the people you are following.

On the homepage, click on **'Following'** to review those you are following. **Decide whether there is anyone you want to stop following.** To 'unfollow', simply put the mouse over the blue **'Following'** button; it turns into a red **'Unfollow'** button which you can click.

Users do NOT get notified of your decision to unfollow them. If you unfollow someone by mistake, simply re-follow them.

Summary of day two

- You have added some followers.
- You have reviewed current conversations.
- You have reviewed comments by those you follow.
- You have sent a few tweets of your own.
- You have sent a few retweets or made some comments.
- You have checked whether anyone's talking about you, or to you, on Twitter.
- You have taken a look at who is following you and followed some back.
- You have taken a look at people you follow and may have stopped following someone.

3 Twitter aids

1. Twitter Help. If you've got a problem with Twitter, don't forget to use the help function. You can find it on the drop-down menu from the cog or wheel icon at the top right of Twitter pages. Alternatively, go directly to support.twitter.com. Twitter Help covers a wide range of problems and features, and is very easy to navigate.

2. Find out what's happening. The **'#Discover'** option on the Twitter menu (top left of the page) will introduce you to leading stories, suggestions of who you should follow, and much more.

3. Keyboard shortcuts. Not all of us like to use the mouse all the time. There is a list of useful keyboard shortcuts on the drop-down menu, accessed through the cog or wheel icon at the top right of Twitter pages.

4 random Twitter facts

1. Tweets per second. On average, 5,700 tweets are posted every second of every day. The highest ever number of tweets per second was 143,199 on 3 August 2013, caused by the reaction to a television programme in Japan.

2. One Direction leads the way. If you believe in such things, a survey by a leading organisation says that One Direction are the most influential people on Twitter in the UK. But I don't follow them.

3. #royalbaby was a top hashtag for 2013. Hashtags often reflect current affairs. On 22 July 2013 Twitter exploded with tweets carrying the hashtags #royalbaby, #royalbabywatch and, later in the day, #royalbabyboy.

The safe arrival of Prince George, firstborn of the Duke and Duchess of Cambridge, was a global news event. On that day alone, the #royalbaby hashtag appeared in over 900,000 tweets.

4. At least one a day. If you think that the layout of your Twitter screen keeps changing slightly, or new features seem to come and go, you're not imagining things. In September 2013 Twitter said on their blog: "It's rare for a day to go by when we're not releasing at least one experiment." The technical wizards in Twitter love to test new features on a group of Twitter users, and that could include you.

Case study four: @berkybear

Twitter delivers nationwide for leaflet distributor

It was a logical step for Mark and Ruth, who run a marketing, leaflet distribution and local magazine business, to get involved with Twitter. Their operation spans the country and their first impression of Twitter was that it had the potential to spread their messages faster than ever.

They started using Twitter in 2011. Their early steps involved learning how hashtags worked and following Twitter users in their immediate area. They soon started retweeting others and getting involved in conversations. Within three months, the @berkybear account had over 1,000 followers. Their first impressions of Twitter's potential were being proved right.

Mark and Ruth's account breaks some of the rules that social media marketers (me included) encourage users to stick to. The first is to give the account a name that connects with the business, but what has @berkybear got to do with local advertising? He's a character (a toy bear) who turns up in their publications, but at first glance it's a curious name for a commercial Twitter account.

The second rule they break is not using a picture of themselves as their profile image. People buy from people and it's generally agreed that a personal picture makes it easier for followers to connect with you. Mark and Ruth's approach is different. They use a cover image from one of their magazines (usually featuring an attractive young lady) as their profile picture.

Despite not adhering to the usual conventions, the @berkybear account is hugely successful, with over 60,000 followers. It's now responsible for generating around 65% of Mark and Ruth's business.

How does @berkybear use Twitter?

Because Twitter is so important to the Look in Local business, it demands a lot of time. Mark and Ruth invest at least three hours every day in reviewing their followers, looking for new people to follow and tweeting.

Their approach is very disciplined. Because they travel around the UK, they tend to focus their Twitter activities on the region they're currently in. Impressively, everything they do is manual (that is, without using any Twitter aids such as Hootsuite or Tweetdeck), because they want to retain the personal approach. Much of their tweeting is from a smartphone.

They value etiquette, maintaining a policy of following back tweeters they consider to be genuine, and in turn, they expect others to return the compliment. Every few months they review who they're following, removing accounts that seem to be inactive.

They also established #satchatUK, an informal gathering of tweeters on a Saturday morning, allowing chat and networking across the country.

How do you choose who to follow on Twitter?

@berkybear follows Twitter accounts based on their geography or industry, and also follows tweeters who they feel add value to their timeline.

Key statistics for @berkybear	
Twitter account opened:	19 August 2011
Number of followers:	Over 74,300
@berkybear follows:	Over 65,600
Number of tweets since August 2011:	Over 51,200
Average number of tweets per day:	53

Day three

Step 1: Repeat steps 1-4 from yesterday, which includes everything from days one and two.

• Add some new followers.

• Review current conversations and comments by those you follow.

• Send a few tweets.

• Send a few retweets or make some comments.

• Check whether anyone's talking about you, or to you, on Twitter.

• Take a look at anyone new who is following you and see if you want to follow them back.

• Take a look at people you follow and see if you want to stop following anyone.

You've probably spotted the trend. Each day builds on what you did before. By now it's becoming a routine that you don't need to be reminded about.

Step 2: Use hashtags in tweets.

If you have not already begun using hashtags, now is the time to start.

A hashtag is a word, or phrase, prefixed with the '#' symbol.

Hashtags are often used to connect tweets to a common theme, such as #olympics or #election or to express emotion, such as #happy.

When you see a hashtag on a tweet, you can click on it to see a list of other recent tweets using that same tag.

Let's say you want to follow what people are saying about a current news story, such as the birth of the royal baby in the UK. You carry out a search on the term 'royal baby' and you spot that many of the tweeters are using the hashtag #royalbaby. By clicking on that hashtag in any tweet, you immediately see the current tweets that also use that hashtag.

There are lots of different uses for hashtags. One popular hashtag is #FollowFriday or #FF. Tweeters use this on Fridays to recommend Twitter accounts to each other.

Feel free to experiment with some hashtags in tweets. Use them to give an indication of how you are feeling or to show the profession or industry about which you are tweeting.

For example, I might tweet: "I am researching types of brick for a client's blog post #copywriting #dull."

In this example, I am tweeting about what I am doing, while the hashtags indicate why I'm doing it (I'm engaged in copywriting) and give a clue as to what I think of it.

(Of course, I would never send a tweet like this, just in case my client spotted it. I never want my clients to think that their projects are dull).

Step 3: Look for someone who needs help in your area of expertise.

A great way to make new contacts on Twitter is by helping someone to solve a problem or find an answer.

To find people who might appreciate your assistance, perform searches using terms such as "Can anyone recommend...?" or "How do I find a good...?".

You are not looking for people to whom you can sell your services. Rather, you want to find people to whom you can give advice. You have expert knowledge in your field of business, so share some.

At the very least, if it seems that someone could use some help, offer to assist. You're not committing to sacrificing hours of your time, but letting them know you're willing to give out some advice in your area of expertise.

An example of a tweet offering assistance is: "@andrew_writer Do you still need help with the MacBook problem? I'm a Mac user and happy to share tips."

This tweet is addressed to @andrew_writer. Remember that when a tweet begins with a Twitter name, its visibility is limited to that person and anyone else who follows both of you.

Information sharing in this way helps to boost your credibility and widen your network.

Summary of day three

- You have added some followers.

- You have reviewed current conversations.

- You have reviewed comments by those you follow.

- You have sent a few tweets of your own.

- You have sent a few retweets or made some comments.

- You have checked whether anyone's talking about you, or to you, on Twitter.

- You have taken a look at who is following you and followed some back.

- You have taken a look at people you follow and may have stopped following someone.

- You have begun to use hashtags.

- You may have offered assistance to someone who needs help.

5 reasons for using Twitter for business

1. Networking. Twitter allows you to make contact with people and organisations in a way that wasn't possible before. Within a matter of months, with careful use of Twitter, you could be talking to some of the leading influencers in your market or area of expertise.

2. Partnership and alliance building. Through building relationships with others in your sphere of interest, you can uncover opportunities for cooperation and collaboration that you never thought were possible.

3. Customer service. Consumers are increasingly using social media channels, such as Facebook and Twitter, to talk with those they buy from. But be warned, customers can access these systems 24/7 and they won't be happy if they have to wait days to get a reply.

4. Market research. Through Twitter, you can spot trends, see what others are talking about and ask questions of current or potential customers. It can be a great way to get the insights and feedback needed to shape your products and services.

5. Marketing. Are you surprised that this is at the bottom, not the top, of this list? That's partly because everything above is also part of marketing, which is all about building awareness of your brand on Twitter. If all you do with Twitter is bombard customers with sales messages, don't be surprised that your follower numbers remain low.

Case study five: @apbassetts

A tweeting West Country solicitor

For a small High Street law firm based in Lostwithiel, Cornwall, A P Bassetts has a big voice on Twitter. They're followed by over 6,000 people and are well-regarded in the small business Twitter community.

The power behind the tweets comes from Joy Bassett, one of the handful of staff in the business. She was introduced to Twitter three years ago by a former employee and began tweeting about issues relevant to their local community. Joy says that almost every business in Lostwithiel uses Twitter.

Joy's Twitter style is friendly and sharing. Her supportive tweets span a diverse range of businesses across the UK, with an inevitable bias towards the legal profession and Cornwall, but encompassing many others besides.

Blogging and tweeting go hand-in-hand, according to Joy. Blogging provides content that can be shared through Twitter, and this content demonstrates A P Bassetts' expertise and capability.

This strategy has been successful. Relationships fostered through Twitter conversations have turned into business for Bassetts. That said, their focus and preference remains a local, face-to-face clientele.

The time management problem

Like most other small firms using social media, time is the biggest barrier to maintaining a consistently strong presence on Twitter. Tools such as Hootsuite and SocialBro help Joy overcome this, with scheduled tweets and tools to manage followers.

Another time-saving technique for gaining followers and encouraging engagement is joining in Twitter networks. A P Bassetts was an early member of the #bizitalk network, a community of small firms centred on Twitter.

How do you choose who to follow on Twitter?

@apbassetts follows other small businesses with accounts on Twitter. Before clicking 'Follow', Joy takes a moment to look at their profile image and text, and to read their last few tweets. If there's evidence of engagement, a willingness to share and chat with fellow tweeters, she's more inclined to follow them.

CASE STUDY FIVE: @APBASSETTS

Key statistics for @apbassetts	
Twitter account opened:	30 September 2010
Number of followers:	Over 6,000
@apbassetts follows:	Over 6,500
Number of tweets since September 2010:	Over 40,600
Average number of tweets per day:	29

6 ways to attract more Twitter followers

Everyone wants more Twitter followers. Some people become obsessed by it, checking their numbers daily, even hourly. After all, the more followers you have, the more influence you exert, or at least, that's the theory.

Here are some suggestions on how to encourage others to follow you on Twitter:

1. Share links to useful or interesting content. This does not mean just posting lots of links to your own website. By sharing useful resources with your followers, you're demonstrating a willingness to help, and that increases the likelihood of others following you.

2. Post frequently. It's up to you how often you post messages on Twitter. But as with the offline world, if people don't see you, most will forget you. Tweeting at least once or twice a day is a recommended minimum, and 5-10 times is better. Of course, if you get into a conversation, you could tweet much more than that in a short space of time, which isn't a problem.

3. Be open and be real. In the same way that most of us rarely warm to a corporation, so Twitter users are not likely to find a bland and seemingly faceless tweeting style attractive. If you're not sure how much of the 'real you' to share, watch what other tweeters do and you should soon find a level of openness that you're comfortable with.

4. Follow others. Don't be afraid to follow anyone you think might be interesting. All Twitter users like to get more followers. Some of those you follow are likely to follow you back. Remember, if having followed someone for a short while you change your mind about them, hitting the 'Unfollow' button is really easy.

5. Share tips. Don't be afraid to let others benefit from your knowledge and insights. Again, being generous with what you share should make you more attractive to others.

6. Answer questions. In the early days of your Twitter use, you could search out questions which you can then answer, as this will increase your visibility and credibility. As you become more established, you may have questions directed at you specifically.

Day four

Step 1: Repeat steps 1-3 from yesterday, which includes everything from days one to three.

You don't have to follow every step in order. By now you should be reasonably confident at navigating around the Twitter pages and tabs.

- Add some new followers.
- Review current conversations and comments by those you follow.
- Send a few tweets.
- Send a few retweets or make some comments.
- Check whether anyone's talking about you, or to you, on Twitter.
- Take a look at anyone new who is following you and see if you want to follow them back.
- Take a look at people you follow and see if you want to stop following anyone.
- Think about using hashtags.
- Consider offering assistance to someone who needs help.

Step 2: Create a list of tweeters.

A list is a useful way of grouping tweeters who are connected by a common theme. You could group them by what they do (e.g. writers), by where they are based, or by some other attribute.

Many power-tweeters say lists are an invaluable tool.

Why create a list? There are several reasons, including:

- To filter the tweets you want to look at. You can choose to view the tweets posted only by those on a list, that either you or someone else has set up.

- To group together particular tweeters. It's a useful way to bookmark or organise specific tweeters.

- To create a Twitter resource. A list can be a source of reference to other Twitter users, such as a list of all the restaurants in your local area who have Twitter accounts.

To get to lists, click on **'Me'** and the last option on the right-hand side under the header is **'More'**. Click on this and choose **'Lists'** from the drop-down menu. You should now see a list of 'Lists' that you are subscribed to, with the option to switch to a list of those which you are a member of. To the right there is also a 'Create new list' button.

Click on **'Create new list'**. This will bring up a box asking for the list name and description and the option to make the list public or private.

For example, say you wanted to create a list of those who regularly tweet quotations. The list title might simply be 'Quotes' and you can enter a description if this is helpful to you. Once the list is created, you can populate it by choosing relevant tweeters. You can add any tweeter to a list, even those you don't follow.

Lists can be very useful as the number of people you follow grows, because lists act as filters, enabling you to look at the tweets from one particular group of tweeters at a time.

You have the option to make lists private, for your own personal use, or to make them public, making them visible to other tweeters, who may find them to be a useful resource.

If you make your lists public, other tweeters can choose to subscribe to them.

Some Twitter users find lists to be an incredibly powerful tool for managing their Twitter activities, while others don't use lists at all.

Step 3: Subscribe to a list.

Subscribing to a list allows you to view it from your own Twitter profile pages. It also indicates your interest to the list owner.

From your homepage or profile page, click on **'Following'** to bring up the list of people you are following. Click on any of these people to bring up their full profile page. If you click on their **'Lists'** tab, this will bring up the lists that they are subscribed to or you can switch to lists that they are members of.

Click on a list name that sounds relevant to your interests. On the list page, you can view a list of members and see the latest tweets. If you want to subscribe, click on the '**Subscribe**' button. This will then be added to your lists page under 'Subscribed to'. This now works in the same way as a list you have created yourself, filtering the tweets to only those from members of that list.

Another way of finding lists that you may want to subscribe to (after you have been on Twitter a while) is by using the 'Member of' tab on the 'Lists' page. This shows you lists that have added you as a member. You may want to subscribe to one of these lists as they are likely to include tweeters who are of interest to you.

Step 4: Favourite a tweet.

You can create a list of your favourite tweets, allowing you to refer back to them later. This could be useful if you spot a tweet which contains information you want to be able to find again easily.

To mark a tweet as a favourite, click the '**Favorite**' option displayed beneath it.

You can access your favourite tweets by clicking '**Me**' and then choosing '**Favorites**' from the list of options displayed. 'Favorites' is a very useful way of keeping a list of helpful information and links.

Do you want to know whenever someone marks one of your tweets as a favourite? If you go to 'Settings' and 'Email Notifications' you'll see there is an option to receive an email whenever someone favourites your tweet.

Summary of day four

- You have added some followers.

- You have reviewed current conversations.

- You have reviewed comments by those you follow.

- You have sent a few tweets of your own.

- You have sent a few retweets or made some comments.

- You have checked whether anyone's talking about you, or to you, on Twitter.

- You have taken a look at who is following you and followed some back.

- You have taken a look at people you follow and may have stopped following someone.

- You have begun to use hashtags.

- You may have offered assistance to someone who needs help.

- You have created a list to organise some of the people you are following.

- You have subscribed to a list.

- You have favourited a tweet.

7 things not to do on Twitter

1. Avoid sending 'check out my website' DMs (direct messages). Most Twitter users don't enjoy receiving self-promotional direct messages, or DMs. Resist the temptation to send your followers individual tweets inviting them to look at your website or to 'Like' your page on Facebook.

2. Don't tweet in anger or haste or both. Because that's when you may tweet something that gets you into trouble. Linger over the 'Tweet' button, taking a moment to consider the implications of what you have written. Will everyone read it in the same 'tone' as you? What you think of as quirky or humorous might cause waves elsewhere, and what impact might that have on your reputation?

3. Don't use Twitter as a one-way channel. Twitter, as with all social media, works best when it's interactive. Some organisations just pump out messages and seem to take no interest in the replies that other tweeters send them.

4. Do not leave your bio or profile picture blank. Those few words and that tiny picture summarise your character on Twitter. Use them wisely.

5. Avoid linking your Twitter account to other social media systems... without being aware of the consequences. Joining everything up can seem like a great time-saver - you can post one message on Twitter, Facebook, LinkedIn, Google+ - just by pressing a single button. But what is that really going to achieve? You may want to use each network for slightly different purposes and a message that's right for one may not be appropriate for another.

6. Do not tweet links without any explanatory text. It might seem clever to send out a tweet containing only a shortened link to a website, but most of your followers will ignore it and some may even think your account has been hacked. If you want someone to click on a link, tell them why.

7. Don't let anyone tell you 'it's wrong to do that on Twitter'. Yes, I know this contradicts everything above. All the points I've listed are personal dislikes of mine, which are shared by many other Twitter users. But there really are no 'rules' on Twitter - if it works for you, then do it. Provided it is legal, that is. Otherwise it could get you into trouble. And even then, never forget that someone, somewhere, might not like what you do.

Case study six: @welshroyalcryst

A historic business succeeds through Twitter

Welsh Royal Crystal is a wonderful example of a historic firm embracing and succeeding with digital communication. Twitter networking has won, and continues to win, significant new business opportunities for the Welsh firm.

Crystal glass has been made in Britain for centuries. Today only three manufacturers remain, and only one of these is in Wales, the small firm of Welsh Royal Crystal. In early 2011, when the previous owner retired, the firm was sold to two employees, David Thomas and Alan O'Neill.

David's wife, Kim, a stay-at-home mother up to that point, took on the challenge of promoting the firm online and she soon discovered Twitter.

In October 2011, she took her tentative first steps on the social network, spending a lot of time watching what others were doing, and learning, by trial and error, how to build a network of contacts.

Two events helped secure the small firm's existence at a time when sales of luxury products were struggling. Firstly, within weeks of its new owners taking over, the company was asked to produce the official Welsh wedding gift for Prince William and Kate Middleton.

Secondly, in March 2012, Kim's tweeting led to the company being recognised and promoted by entrepreneur Theo Paphitis in his weekly #SBS competition. The ongoing relationship between the ex-Dragon's Den panellist and Welsh Royal Crystal has helped the firm win several important contracts and given it a high profile in the national press.

There's no doubt that Twitter has helped the company secure its future and grow revenue.

How does @WelshRoyalCryst use Twitter?

Kim is the only person in the business who operates Twitter, or indeed knows how to use it. She's built a strong following of fans and customers through a high level of engagement, although her time spent on Twitter is less now than it was a year or so back.

Tools such as Hootsuite, twitNERD and Unfollowers.me are valuable productivity aids to Kim, providing tweet scheduling and follower management.

Kim has made a point of learning how her Twitter community works. She knows the time of day when people are most likely to ask questions about products and making orders. She's also spent a lot of time understanding Google analytics and can track how a click on a tweeted link converts into a sale.

Using Twitter for customer service is, Kim believes, the key to their success. She responds to enquiries quickly, converting many of them into sales.

What's changed since 2013?

@WelshRoyalCryst was a case study in the previous, 2013, edition of this book. The big change in the last twelve months has been Kim's very conscious decision to cut down her time on Twitter.

The social network remains very important to the business, but it was getting out of control. Her high visibility led to numerous requests for help, sucking up that most precious of resources - time.

By taking a short break from Twitter and then re-engaging, but with stricter terms of what she would allow herself to do, Kim ensures her networking remains focused on what's good for the business.

How do you choose who to follow on Twitter?

Genuine engagement is very important to Kim. Before following someone, she takes a look at their profile and reads their most recent tweets, only clicking 'Follow' if she likes what she sees.

Unlike many on Twitter, Kim also actively manages her list of followers, blocking those she considers to be unsuitable. She gets comments about the high quality of following for the @WelshRoyalCryst account, so she knows people are looking at her follower list.

CASE STUDY SIX: @WELSHROYALCRYST

Key statistics for @WelshRoyalCryst

Twitter account opened:	12 October 2011
Number of followers:	Over 12,800
@WelshRoyalCryst follows:	Over 11,000
Number of tweets since October 2011:	Over 109,000
Average number of tweets per day:	142

8 uses for Twitter

1. Talk to suppliers. Along with many others, I use Twitter to reach the big companies I buy from. My broadband supplier, supermarket and DVD rental company have all responded to complaints I have made on Twitter. It can be a very fast route to a customer service team.

2. Check the weather. If you want to know if it's raining, snowing or sunny in a specific place, you can probably find out from Twitter. If no one is tweeting about it right now, ask the question.

3. Travel news updates. Twitter is a great source of real-time news about road closures, rail delays and problems at airports. Use the Twitter search function to look up the road name or place that you are interested in.

4. Get special offers. Many firms run special deals, and even giveaways, on Twitter. Keep your eyes open because there are some fantastic deals to be had.

5. Find out what's going on at an event. An increasing number of conferences, exhibitions and other big events are using a common hashtag to connect all the tweets about the event. If you follow the tweets using that hashtag, the many tweeters using it will give you a great feel for what's going on.

6. Get answers to questions. Twitter gives you access to hundreds of thousands of people, through various levels of followers. If you have a specific question, there's a good chance you can get an answer through Twitter, or at least be put in touch with someone who can help.

7. Build a network of specialists. Within minutes of opening a Twitter account, you could be following a host of experts in your chosen field. Using the search function, and then seeing who follows who, you can discover specialists from across the world.

8. Have fun. Homeworkers often describe Twitter as the place they go for coffee-break banter. Whatever time of day you go onto Twitter, there will be someone to talk to and humour to entertain.

Day five

Step 1: Repeat steps 1-4 from yesterday, which includes everything from days one to four.

- Add some new followers.

- Review current conversations and comments by those you follow.

- Send a few tweets.

- Send a few retweets or make some comments.

- Check whether anyone's talking about you, or to you, on Twitter.

- Take a look at anyone new who is following you and see if you want to follow them back.

- Take a look at people you follow and see if you want to stop following anyone.

- Think about using hashtags.

- Consider offering assistance to someone who needs help.

- Consider making a list to organise some of the people you are following.

- Consider subscribing to a list.

- See if there are any tweets you want to mark as favourites.

By now you should be feeling reasonably confident with Twitter. You're starting to establish patterns - such as when to fit tweeting into your schedule, your style of tweeting and the type of conversation you like to join in.

Step 2: Take a look at what's trending.

If you haven't already noticed, there's a section marked **'Trends'** on every Twitter page. In the current layout, it's on the left-hand side of the Twitter page, except on the profile page, where it's on the right. This displays the most popular topics on Twitter at the moment, some of which may use hashtags. These trends are tailored based on your location and the people you follow.

To see tweets containing the word or phrase, simply click on it. As an alternative to tailored trends, you can look at trends at a worldwide, national or regional level - click on **'Change'** to see the options.

A trend marked 'Promoted' has been sponsored. It is a form of advertising.

Step 3: Pin a tweet.

A new feature of Twitter, introduced in April 2014, is the ability to 'pin' a tweet on your profile page. Pinning a tweet keeps it in a fixed position at the top of the list of your tweets displayed to people looking at your profile.

To pin a tweet, select **'...'** ('More') from the options displayed beneath each tweet and choose **'Pin to your profile page'**. You can only pin your own tweets.

Why would you pin a tweet? Perhaps it contains information, or a picture, that you're keen for others to see. Maybe you think it's particularly funny or clever. It's your choice whether or not to pin a tweet.

You can only have one pinned tweet at a time. When you select a new tweet to pin, the previously pinned tweet is removed.

Step 4: Search for information on Twitter.

Searching tweets can reveal opportunities for business, potential new contacts, and useful information. A search can give insights into topics that others are discussing, and make you aware of issues you hadn't previously considered.

Twitter is becoming a popular search engine, with over two billion searches being carried out daily.

As with any search, to be effective, you need to know what you are looking for.

However, a good way to gain a feel for Twitter search is to start with something general. In the **'Search'** box at the top of the page, type in your job title, such as 'copywriter' or 'website designer'.

The search brings back a list of people and tweet that match those words. The basic rules of search apply: type in 'marketing manager' (without the speech or quotation marks), and you'll see every tweet with both those words in it, but not necessarily in that order.

However, put speech or quotation marks around a phrase and the search will find tweets containing that exact text.

Once you are in the search area, you can choose to search everything or limit your search to people, photos, videos or news.

You can also conduct an **'Advanced Search'**. There are a variety of options to choose from relating to the words you want to appear, or not appear, in the tweet, the accounts you want Twitter to search and the place you want the tweet to originate. It also gives you the opportunity to exclude retweets and look for whether the tweet includes '?', ':)' or ':('.

Summary of day five

- You have added some followers.

- You have reviewed current conversations.

- You have reviewed comments by those you follow.

- You have sent a few tweets of your own.

- You have sent a few retweets or made some comments.

- You have checked whether anyone's talking about you, or to you, on Twitter.

- You have taken a look at who is following you and followed some back.

- You have taken a look at people you follow and may have stopped following someone.

- You have begun to use hashtags.

- You may have offered assistance to someone who needs help.

- You may have created or subscribed to a list.

- You may have favourited a tweet.

- You have learned how to see what's trending.

- You have pinned a tweet.

- You have learned how to use Twitter search as a basis for engaging with others.

9 different types of tweet

1. A standard tweet contains up to 140 characters. It could be as simple as: "I've just had a fantastic meeting with my boss."

2. A mention tweet includes the name of at least one other Twitter user: "I've just had a fantastic meeting with @rachel_writer_, my boss."

3. A 'reply' tweet starts with someone's Twitter name: "@rachel_writer_ Thanks for the fantastic meeting."
Important: Remember that a reply tweet is not sent to all your followers. It is sent to the person named at the start of the tweet, and any follower of yours who is also a follower of theirs. However, your tweet is not private and is visible to anyone performing a search, or looking at the tweets you have sent.

4. A direct message is a private tweet, visible only to the recipient. As a general rule, you can only send a direct message to someone who follows you, although some accounts now accept direct messages from anyone: "@rachel_writer_ I appreciate you taking the time to help with those work issues."

5. A retweet is where you forward to your followers a tweet sent by someone else.

6. A thank you tweet is where you thank another tweeter for doing something, such as retweeting one of your messages, or sharing some useful advice or information. There is no obligation to say 'thank you', but it's polite.

7. A sharing tweet contains a link to a useful or entertaining website. Long links are often shortened automatically by Twitter or other tweeting tools: "I've just had a fantastic meeting with my boss who recommended this website http:// ow.ly/auvDM."

8. A hashtag tweet contains a hashtag, which is simply a way of tagging a tweet with potentially useful information or emotion: "I've just had a fantastic meeting with my boss #appraisal #payrise #yippee."

9. A spam tweet. From time to time you'll get a tweet with your name at the front, often a fairly random comment, and a link. If the tweet's from a stranger, **don't click on the link**. It is quite probably going to take you to somewhere unpleasant.

Case study seven: @RegencyHistory

A tweeter who followed the Twitter Action Plan

RegencyHistory.net is a blog about Regency and late Georgian history written by my wife, Rachel. I encouraged her to try using Twitter to promote her blog and build an audience for her work.

Rachel started to use Twitter in January 2012 using the Twitter Action Plan as her guide. She is very familiar with the guide having edited the content as it has been developed. I have had no hands-on involvement in her Twitter account.

In the first year, she gained 1000 followers and after two years, she has over 3000.

How does @RegencyHistory use Twitter?

Rachel uses Hootsuite to schedule tweets but also usesTwitter.com and the Twitter app on the iPad. She tweets links to posts on her blog at varying times of the day and retweets messages, usually about history or writing, which she thinks will be of interest to her followers. She always clicks on a link to check that it works before retweeting and makes sure that her own tweets link to the right page.

She has created lists of her favourite tweeters and their tweets appear in separate columns on Hootsuite which she can easily scan to see if there is anything she wants to retweet.

Rachel tries to reply to everyone who asks her a question or comments on her tweets and thanks people who retweet her.

Her tweets generate a high number of click-throughs from Twitter to her blog posts and Facebook page.

What's changed since 2013?

@RegencyHistory was a case study in the previous edition of this book.

Rachel has continued to use Twitter nearly every day in 2013 and has seen her follower numbers increase to over 3000.

How do you choose who to follow on Twitter?

Rachel mainly follows other writers and historians and those whose tweets would be of interest to her followers.

She looks for a profile picture and a bio that indicates an interest in history, writing or reading. She also looks at the last few tweets to ensure that the account has been used recently, that they do not contain anything offensive and they are not purely self-promotional.

CASE STUDY SEVEN: @REGENCYHISTORY

Rachel reviews new followers to see if she wants to follow back. She also reviews tweets full of Twitter names, which are either thanking them for retweeting or #FF recommendations, sent by tweeters she trusts, to consider whether to follow them.

Key statistics for @RegencyHistory

Twitter account opened: 4 January 2012
Number of followers: Over 3,400
@RegencyHistory follows: Over 2,900
Number of tweets
since January 2012:   Over 7,900
Average number of
tweets per day: 7

---

10 things you need to remember about Twitter

1. Please try to avoid this common mistake. **If you want a tweet to be visible to all your followers, do not start it with a Twitter user name.** Any tweet that starts with a user name is directed to that person, and to any followers you have in common. It's not a private message, but neither is it published to all your followers.

2. Do not assume that because you've sent a tweet, your followers have read it. You might read all the tweets coming your way, but that's because you're a Twitter newbie. Once you're following 500+ people, you won't read anywhere near all the messages they send out.

3. You can delete tweets after sending them, but it's likely that some people will have already read them. **It's better to hesitate before hitting 'Send' rather than regretting and deleting.** Twitter will probably store undeleted tweets forever.

4. Twitter is fundamentally a public communication channel. If you're really bothered about privacy, be careful how you use it, or don't use it at all.

5. It's good to be polite. It's perfectly okay to thank Twitter users for retweeting your messages. A simple "Thanks for the RT" or "Thanks for the kind retweet" can help build a positive relationship with your fellow tweeters. But don't take offence if you are not always thanked for your retweets.

6. Some Twitter accounts are marked as 'verified', particularly celebrity accounts. This means you can trust that they are who they claim to be. Although it may be their staff who are doing the tweeting.

7. No one 'owns' a hashtag '#'. Anyone can start using one and encourage others to use it. They're a great way of connecting conversations on a common theme.

8. Sadly, spammers and hackers love Twitter. **If you're invited to click on a link and you have the slightest doubt about the sender or if the message looks out of character, DON'T CLICK!**

9. There are two styles of retweet. The first effectively forwards the entire tweet, and it appears on the timeline as being from the original sender, although a small note will indicate who retweeted it.

The second usually starts 'RT' and contains the original text, with perhaps a comment. To do this from Twitter.com requires you to cut, paste and edit. Systems such as Hootsuite give you the choice of retweet styles.

10. Twitter can stop or change its service, permanently or temporarily, without any warning. Make sure that you have thought about how you or your business would cope without Twitter.

Twitter and your mobile phone

Six out of ten tweeters read and send tweets through their smartphone or tablet, and many of them prefer this to logging in from a 'proper' computer.

To get the almost full Twitter experience on your mobile requires downloading the Twitter app for your Apple, Android, Blackberry or Windows phone. Why 'almost full'? Because not all Twitter functions, particularly 'Settings', are available on mobile devices.

In addition, you can increasingly enjoy the Twitter experience without using an app and without internet access, by using text messaging. The first step to activate this is to tell Twitter your mobile phone number in **'Settings'** then **'Mobile'**.

Before rushing to turn on all the text messaging features Twitter allows, remember that you may be paying for some of these. It all depends on your contract with your mobile provider. Don't blame Twitter (or me) if you run up a big bill!

Note that you can only link your mobile phone number with one Twitter account.

Receive updates via text

You can choose to receive notifications of Twitter events via text message. These include:

• Direct messages

• When someone new follows you

• When you are mentioned in a tweet

• When someone replies to your tweet

The full list of options can be found in 'Settings' under the 'Mobile' tab.

You can also choose to receive the tweets sent by specific tweeters via text message, by choosing to turn on mobile notifications from them. When their profile is displayed, select the cog icon and choose **'Turn on mobile notifications'**. Turning it off is just as easy.

To make mobile notifications via text more user-friendly, Twitter allows you to specify certain hours when they won't be sent. This means you can leave your phone on all night without being woken by the continual buzz or 'ding' of messages coming in.

Send messages via text

When you activate Twitter on your mobile, you'll be sent a text message. Make a note of the number this message comes from, because this is the number you can use to tweet via text and to control a variety of other functions.

Sending a tweet via text is very easy. Simply type your text in the same way you would write a tweet and send it.

The message will go to all your followers, just as a regular tweet would, and it will appear in your timeline.

That's not the end of it. You can retweet, send Direct Messages, follow and unfollow, mark tweets as favourites and even view another user's Twitter statistics (how many they follow and follow them), all from a mobile phone via text messaging.

The full list of commands and options is on the Twitter support pages, under 'Twitter SMS Commands'. Here's a selection of the most useful.

I have written all the commands in upper case, as that's the way they appear on the Twitter support page, but my experience is that they are not case sensitive.

OFF: Disables all Twitter notifications to your mobile phone. If you want to reactivate them, choose ON.

ON [username]: Turns on text notifications of tweets from a specific user, such as 'ON andrew_writer'. Twitter says not to use the '@' symbol when writing user names into command messages, because it could confuse the messaging system, but I have found that commands with or without '@' both work for me.

FOLLOW [username]: This allows you to follow someone new and it automatically turns on text notifications. This command can be abbreviated to F [username].

OFF [username]: Turns off text notifications from a user.

UNFOLLOW [username]: Unfollows the specific Twitter account.

D [username] + message: Sends a direct message to a specific Twitter user.

@[username] + message: Sends a 'reply' tweet.

SET BIO: The content of your text message becomes your Twitter bio.

RETWEET [username]: Retweets the last tweet sent by the user you are referring to, such as RETWEET [andrew_writer]. This can be shortened to RT [username].

GET [username]: Tells you the last tweet sent by that user.

STATS [username]: Tells you how many people someone follows, how many follow them and also supplies their bio.

This is just a short list of the most useful commands available for Twitter via text messaging. It's a very powerful system and could be very useful if you find yourself wanting to tweet when you have no internet access.

How to protect your Twitter account from being hacked

As you build your Twitter account, it will develop value. Whether you use it for personal or business tweeting, or both, that value is not measured in pounds and pence (or dollars and cents). It's measured in trust. Many of your followers trust what you say, and it's this trust that hackers want to steal.

Hackers want to send out messages in your name, in the hope that your followers will believe them to be from you. These messages usually contain links to websites promoting products they want to sell and which may also contain malware - viruses that download the moment someone visits the website.

Not all hackers are distant and faceless. Your account could also be hacked by someone closer to home, like a friend, family member or someone from work or school. You may have shared your password with them, or worse, your password might be very easy to guess.

How to spot a Twitter hack

If you think your Twitter account has been hacked, take a look at the Direct Messages (DMs) that have recently gone out from it. You can access your DMs by clicking on the envelope symbol to the right of the search bar at the top of each Twitter page. Here you'll see the most recent DMs sent and received.

If you didn't write the outgoing DMs, your account has been hacked.

Other evidence of being hacked is that someone has added or removed followers, or blocked followers.

Preventing hacking is always better than curing it and these tips will help you to better protect the value in your Twitter account, by making it harder for hackers to break in.

1. Check you're using a genuine login page.

One method hackers use to snare passwords is to send out spam emails asking users to re-enter their account name and password. The email contains a link to what looks like a genuine Twitter login page but is actually a fake.

To get around this, bookmark the genuine Twitter login page on your browser and only go to that page via your bookmark. Always be suspicious of links in emails. Read the website address carefully to ensure it really does say https://twitter.com.

2. Distrust any site or app that asks for your password.

The moment you're asked to input your Twitter password into an app or a non-Twitter website, be suspicious. Unless you're confident that the account or app is genuine, you're in danger of giving your password to a hacker.

3. Use a long, clever password.

Most of us hate remembering complicated passwords, which is why so many accounts are easy to break into - we continue to use passwords that are easy to crack.

Twitter's advice is to use a password that's at least 10 characters long and contains upper and lower case letters, numbers and symbols. Don't use complete words.

Long passwords can be daunting, but there are techniques for making them easier to remember.

4. Never use the same password on two accounts.

This is hard, because most of us have so many different accounts. But it's a good habit to get into. As with long passwords, there are techniques for creating unique codes that aren't impossible to remember.

5. Change your password often

On top of creating long, complex passwords, it's wise to update them every few months. It takes a bit of time, but that's nothing to the hours you'll probably spend clearing up the damage after being hacked.

If you use apps that require your Twitter password, these may not work until you input the new password.

6. Use two-step authentication

This is where the Twitter login process requires an extra step to confirm that it really is you trying to get into your account.

You have two choices of two-step authentication method. You can have login verification requests sent either to your mobile by text or to your Twitter app.

Both methods are activated by going to 'Settings', then 'Account' and choosing a login verification method. Login verification by phone means that after entering your Twitter password, you're sent a special code via text message that you also need to type in before being allowed into your Twitter account.

The second two-step method uses the Twitter app you can download to your mobile phone or tablet. When you type in your Twitter password, a notification is sent to the app.

To complete the login process you must accept this notification request, which is also found under the security settings. This request includes information about the location of the person attempting to log in, which could give you a clue as to whether it's a hacker and not you.

The advantages of the app-based two-step process are that it uses strong security technology and it allows access to multiple Twitter accounts to be managed from a single phone. The drawback is that it won't work if your phone or other mobile device is unable to access the internet for any reason.

So what happens if you've turned on two-step authentication but don't have access to your mobile when you want to log in? Twitter has a solution for this - a backup code that you can find using your Twitter app. The idea is that you write down (with a good old pen and paper) this code and put it in a secure place. Look up and use this code if, for whatever reason, you can't complete the two-step process using your mobile device.

7. Never tell anyone your password

Sharing passwords can be quick and convenient. But every password shared is a password at risk of being abused, meaning the safest approach is to keep it secret, always. If circumstances mean you do need to share it, make a point of changing it as soon as possible.

8. Virus and malware protection

Nasty programs that find their way onto your computer can steal your Twitter login details. Protect against these in the same way you defend against other dangerous downloads, using anti-virus software along with a dose of common sense.

How to recover from a Twitter hack

If you're unfortunate enough to have your account hacked, the first action to recover the situation is to change your password.

It's a wise precaution to also change the password on the email account associated with your Twitter account.

If you can't get into the account to change the password, use the password reset option. If you can't even do this, get in touch with Twitter support.

The next step is to revoke permission on some, or all, of the apps you've allowed to access your Twitter account. One of these could well be the source of the hack. Click the 'cog' symbol and choose 'Settings'. Select 'Apps' and revoke access for any app in which you don't have complete trust.

You're now in control of your Twitter account, and identity, again. The next step is to recover from the damage done by the hack, and to do all you can to make sure it doesn't happen again.

How to use the Twitter archive tool

In 2013, Twitter launched a function allowing you to download a list of every tweet you've ever sent.

Until the archive function arrived, the only way of going back to old tweets was to scroll down through your 'Tweets' list on Twitter.com. That's okay if the words you're looking for were sent yesterday, but looking back through several months is painful, if not impossible.

Why would you want a record of all your tweets?

With the impact of the average tweet dying away in seconds, and with so many containing inconsequential nonsense (unless you're up there with the Dalai Lama), where's the value in a record of the probably thousands of tweets that you've sent?

Here's why I might want to go back over my old tweets:

- To find that tweeted photograph that I've failed to keep a copy of anywhere else, despite my best intentions to be a better curator of images.

- To prove to myself, or someone else, that I really did tweet a particular message at a particular time.

- To find that cleverly-worded message I used months ago that it's safe to reuse now, when it might receive more appreciation. Yes, it's lazy to recycle tweets but it happens.

- Purely for the purpose of maintaining a record of all my tweets, just in case I need it.

You can probably think of other reasons why you might want a record of all your tweets.

What does the Twitter archive give you?

The archive puts a copy of all the tweets you've ever sent, including RTs (retweets), onto your computer. The archive does not include DMs (direct messages).

Some thought has gone into the presentation of your Twitter archive, which you access through your browser, even though the information is held on your own computer. The tweets are presented very much as they are on your live Twitter account, with the most recent at the top.

In addition to all your tweets, the archive gives you a visual indicator of the volume of tweets you've sent out each month over the life of your account. This indicator is also a useful navigational tool, allowing you to hop from one month to another.

You're provided with the standard Twitter search box at the top of the page, which now searches all the tweets in your archive, bringing back all those that contain the word or exact phrase you searched for.

How to use the Twitter archive tool

The new archive function is really easy to find. Click on the cog symbol at the top of the page and select **'Settings'**. At the bottom of the 'Account' settings page you will see a section labelled 'Your Twitter Archive'.

Press the big **'Request your archive'** button. You'll be told to wait while the archive is prepared and when that's complete, you'll receive an email to the address linked to that account. This process usually only takes a few moments.

The email will give you another button to press that downloads the archive as a zip (compressed) file. You'll have to unzip, or extract, the contents of the file, into a suitable location on your computer.

Once you've unzipped the file, click on the index.html file to open the archive in your browser, and enjoy reading all those tweets you'd long forgotten that you'd sent.

Twitter and the law

In 2012 over 650 people in England and Wales found themselves facing criminal charges as a result of their tweets and Facebook posts. Many were accused of harassment or making violent threats.

Even if you intend to keep all your Twitter postings friendly and constructive, it pays to have a little understanding of what's inside and outside the law. This knowledge could protect you from making mistakes and from having others take advantage of your rights.

This section is intended only as a guide to some of the issues you should be aware of. Because social media is still very new, there are many areas of law where it remains to be tested.

Copyright

Music, images and text can all be shared at the click of a button. But just because it's easy, does it make it right?

The principle of copyright - where the creator retains ownership of a work - is well-established in law, even if it can become a fiendishly complex issue at times.

This means you own the copyright of every photo you take, even if you choose to share it far and wide on Twitter. However, if it's a newsworthy or eye-catching image, don't be surprised if others share it, often without giving you the credit. Some may decide to share it on other channels, even in print. Some Twitter photos have found their way onto the front of newspapers, without the photographer's explicit permission.

Early in 2013 a US court ruled that the Washington Post and others had infringed the copyright of a freelance photographer by publishing and distributing pictures without permission. The photographer had posted the images on Twitter.

Twitter's terms of service are very clear. While you give them permission to share your content across their network, including partners, you retain ownership.

But it's your job to ensure no one abuses your rights of ownership. It's also up to you to make sure you don't infringe copyright by using material created by others, without their permission.

Harassment, threats and abuse

People do and say things online that they would never do in face-to-face situations. Psychologists call this 'disinhibition' - because people believe they are anonymous, their behaviour becomes unrestrained.

However, as more and more people are taken to court for abusing and threatening others online, it's clear that the apparent anonymity has not protected them from being traced and prosecuted.

We all get annoyed with others from time to time, but it's safer not to convert that frustration into words which, once typed and sent, can never be fully erased.

If you do tweet something unpleasant which you have cause to regret, follow it up with an apology and expression of remorse. This acknowledges that you've stepped over the line and could also offer some protection, should you face legal action.

To help protect tweeters, Twitter have now added a 'Report Tweet' option, found under **'More'** beneath every tweet.

Privacy and libel

Almost half of people aged 18-24 don't realise they can be sued for defamation for sharing, via a tweet, an unsubstantiated rumour about someone.

We all have a right not to be libelled by those around us, including in the online world. The simple act of retweeting a message that contains malicious gossip about someone could be considered libel and could get you into trouble with the law.

As with other copyright and abuse, applying some common sense to your tweeting should offer some protection from invading the privacy or damaging the good name of others via Twitter. Think before you tweet (or retweet) and if you believe there's a risk of causing upset, don't do it.

Some Twitter terms explained

Like every system and community, Twitter has its own special language, of both 'official' terms and community slang.

While many of the terms used have been explained throughout this book, here's a handy reminder of those you're most likely to encounter:

Direct Message (DM): A private tweet that is only visible to the sender and the recipient. You can only send a Direct Message to a tweeter that follows you.

Hashtag: A word or phrase preceded by the '#' symbol. Hashtags are a way of connecting tweets with a common theme.

Mention tweet: A tweet that 'mentions' the name of another Twitter account in the text.

#music: Launched in 2013, this is a specific service that helps people to find new and emerging music through Twitter. To use it, download the #music app or visit music.twitter.com.

SOME TWITTER TERMS EXPLAINED

MT: A tweet that begins MT is a retweet where the text has been modified from the original.

Promoted: From time to time you'll see tweets, accounts or trends marked as 'Promoted'. These are effectively adverts that have been paid for by organisations promoting themselves and their products.

Reply tweet: A tweet that begins with someone's Twitter name, and where the very first character is the '@' symbol. Reply tweets only appear in the timeline of the account they are addressed to, and those of any other tweeters who follow both the sender and recipient. However, these are not private messages and will appear in searches carried out by other tweeters.

RT: A tweet that begins RT is a retweet, and is usually followed by the name of the tweeter who sent the original message.

Trends: These are the words, phrases or hashtags that represent hot topics on Twitter right now. Trends can be viewed at global, national or regional level.

Troll: Some people take delight in harassing others online. This can range from mischievous banter to violent threats. Such people are referred to as trolls and their behaviour as trolling.

SOME TWITTER TERMS EXPLAINED

Tweetdeck: This is a dashboard system owned by Twitter, which allows you to manage one or more Twitter accounts.

Tweetup: Twitter's a great way to make new friends and contacts, and, being human, many of us like to go a step further and meet the people we tweet with. These gatherings, formal and informal, are generally referred to as tweetups.

Twitter jail: Twitter limits how many tweets you can send per day and even per hour. If you exceed these limits, your account is temporarily barred from posting and this is referred to as 'Twitter jail'. The only way to get out of Twitter jail is to wait. You may be able to tweet again within just a few minutes.

Vine: Launched by Twitter in 2013, Vine allows you to create tiny videos (6 seconds long) that loop continuously. To use it, download the Vine app for your mobile device.

Questions people are often too embarrassed to ask

There are lots of Twitter details that even experienced tweeters don't know, and are often too shy to ask because they think they really should know the answer by now.

So here's a list to spare your blushes!

What is a tweep?

Tweep is another word for tweeter – someone who tweets.

If I unfollow someone, does Twitter tell them?

No, Twitter keeps your little secret, although their follower number does drop and if they don't have very many, it might not take long to work out who's gone. There are also lots of third party tools that can let them know, if they bother to ask.

QUESTIONS

What's a third party tool for Twitter?

This is another system which takes information from or posts to Twitter, which is not written by the people who created Twitter. There are lots of tools out there, which people use to help them manage their Twitter account.

One of the most commonly used is Hootsuite, which allows people to manage multiple Twitter accounts very easily, and means they rarely need to log into Twitter.com directly.

However, using a third party system can lose access to some of Twitter's features, such as looking at photos and other media on Twitter itself rather than having to click on a link to another page.

Many third party tools offer a free version and a premium, or paid-for, version of their product.

How do I schedule tweets?

A scheduled tweet is a message that's posted at an assigned time. You can't schedule tweets from Twitter.com; to do this you need a third party tool. There are several offering the capability to schedule tweets, such as Hootsuite and Tweetdeck.

I thought I was following someone, but I'm not. Is my memory playing tricks?

Possibly, although you may have fallen foul of the Twitter unfollow bug. Every now and again, you may stop following a tweeter, despite never having gone anywhere near the 'Unfollow' button.

That's because a bug in Twitter made you unfollow them. It's a problem that Twitter knows about and is working to fix.

Can I pick up a virus through Twitter?

Yes, you can, or more precisely, your computer can. But you can't get an infection simply by reading a tweet; you need to click on a link to make that happen. In the same way that you must take care when clicking on links in emails, only click on Twitter links that you trust, and always be suspicious of links sent by people you normally trust when the message is not in their usual writing style. Be particularly aware of DMs or @yourtwittername messages.

Why can't I follow more than 2,001 people?

Tweeters in a rush to attract lots of followers follow lots of people in the hope that a good number will return the favour. But they hit a brick wall at 2,001.

This is because once you start to follow more than 2,000 Twitter users, the system starts to control how many you can follow, in proportion to how many follow you.

Twitter does not publish how that balance is calculated - and it probably varies depending on who you are - but in my experience, Twitter requires you to have a follower count of at least 90% of the number you follow. In other words, to break the 2,001 barrier, you need at least 1,800 followers of your own.

QUESTIONS

I wish I hadn't posted that tweet, but I can delete it, right?

Yes, you can delete a tweet and it'll be gone forever. But... some people will already have seen it and will remember it. The tweet will remain visible in some third party systems, such as Hootsuite, long after you hit the Delete button.

Some people capture potentially embarrassing tweets by taking a screenshot - an image of their computer display.

What next?

You've reached the end of 'Your Five-day Twitter Action Plan'. It doesn't matter if you've followed the plan daily, done the whole thing in one sitting, or taken weeks.

However, what does matter is how often you repeat what you've learned. Repetition will create a Twitter habit, and, in time, this will build you a following and an online reputation. Continue to use this action plan for as long as you want.

Having got this far, you may have decided that Twitter is not for you. There's nothing wrong with that. You could try other social networks, such as Facebook or Google+.

Or you might prefer other methods of building a network. As in all aspects of business, you'll get the best results from doing what you enjoy and what comes most naturally to you.

There is more to learn about Twitter

Twitter's features and functions are being updated almost every day, meaning that any book, including this one, is out of date even before it is published.

The way we are using Twitter is also changing, as people experiment with new approaches and tools.

This guide has been designed to give you a step-by-step guide through the most important actions in Twitter. It's also covered many features that even experienced tweeters are not particularly aware of. To keep informed about what's new on Twitter, I recommend that you follow me: **@andrew_writer.**

For more hints and tips about using Twitter and other social networks, follow **@5Day_ActionPlan** on Twitter.

Andrew Knowles
Weymouth, Dorset
January 2014

About the author

Andrew Knowles is a professional communicator and an enthusiastic supporter of small businesses.

Having been awarded a degree in Archaeology and History by the University of Southampton, Andrew qualified as an accountant in the early 1990s. But he always preferred words to numbers.

Andrew's enthusiasm for effective communication and process improvement led him into software consultancy and training, where he helped a variety of organisations, large and small, to get the best from their new finance systems.

ABOUT THE AUTHOR

Andrew now works full-time as a writer, speaker and trainer, helping organisations to improve their communication through many channels, including social media. He has written books on social media and a guide to writing an outstanding CV.

He lives in Weymouth, Dorset, England, within a seagull's glide of the Jurassic Coast World Heritage Site.

Index

INDEX

INDEX

www.ingramcontent.com/pod-product-compliance
Lightning Source LLC
Chambersburg PA
CBHW052147070326
40689CB00050B/2423